The Agency Management Handbook

Your Guide to Greater Success and Profitability

DARRYL SALERNO

Second Quadrant Solutions

ISBN: 978-0-578-63396-1

Library of Congress Control Number: 2020900412

Editing, design and production by Joanne Shwed, Backspace Ink (www.backspaceink.com)

Contents

Foreword

I have been in the communications agency business for more than four decades, with the last 20 years as a consultant to more than 100 agencies. Some of those agencies have only a few people; others have several hundred. They have offices all over the United States and overseas. They cover virtually every practice area and discipline.

Despite the huge diversity of the agencies, they all have two things in common: They work too hard and don't make enough money for the effort they put in.

While focusing on the everyday pressures of client issues, agency managers frequently lose sight of the long-term effects on their own business:

- Out of fear of upsetting the client relationship, employees are continually asked to do work that should be done by more junior people.

- Agencies are reluctant to push back when clients ask for activities that were not in, or were very different from, the original scope of work.

- When clients push for a discount on the work being done, many agencies capitulate without considering the effect on other clients and their employees.

- When employees are promoted to supervisory positions, they are rarely trained to be good managers. They are generally promoted based on their client-facing abilities even when they are poor at managing staff or cooperating with peers.

■ At many smaller agencies, owners take much of their compensation at the end of the year. They often believe they are making reasonable profits because they are understating their compensation costs.

I have tried to make it my mission to change the dynamics of agency life by helping them operate as more effective businesses.

Focusing on Where You Want to Go

If you don't know where you're going, you might wind up someplace else.

—Yogi Berra

Vision

- Why are you in business?
- What are you trying to accomplish?
- How will you know if you're successful?

Have you ever asked yourself these questions? Without a clear idea of what you ultimately want your company to be, it is very difficult to make the correct day-to-day decisions because you will find yourself reacting to the exigencies of the moment rather than taking actions that will drive you towards your ultimate goals and the success you desire.

While operating your business each day, you will be faced with questions, problems and opportunities that require your time and attention. How you deal with these situations will determine your progress and performance. Without a firm concept of what you want to achieve in the long term, you may find yourself making decisions that will bring immediate relief but will not help you get where you want to go.

In professional service firms, many of these decisions revolve around acquisition, retention and development of staff. When faced with issues such as allocating resources to make strategic hires, offering compensation for key individuals and providing professional development and coaching for your employees, it is critical to know what you want your company to look like in five or 10 years in order to determine how to proceed.

Without a game plan, you will be making these determinations with an eye only on how it will affect the organization in the immediate future. While this is a criterion for deciding, it is less important than looking at the long-term implications. In fact, in many cases, tomorrow's problems will be created by today's solutions.

As a starting point, you need to decide what you want to achieve personally through your business.

- How much money do you want to make?
- What type of work-life balance do you want to achieve?
- What do you want the perceptions of the company to say about you as an individual?

You should begin the process by writing personal goals that will provide the direction for how you operate within the organization and in your personal life. There are several exercises you might try to help you articulate these goals properly.

One way to focus on this process is to imagine that you have lived to a ripe old age and have just passed away. Write your obituary or the eulogy you would like someone to give on your behalf.

- How do you want to be remembered?
- What will you have accomplished?
- What would constitute the best life you could have led?

For some, this exercise has too great a time horizon. If that is true for you, pick a shorter time frame. Imagine that it is 10 years from today. You have just bumped into a close friend at the airport whom you haven't seen for the past 10 years. You have a minute to embrace and exchange cards before flying home from your business trip. When you arrive home, you find a lengthy e-mail from this friend, describing  everything that has happened in her life over the past 10 years. Write a response that describes your achievements in that period.

The purpose of these exercises is to free your mind of your current situation and to imagine what you would like to achieve over an extended period. Be bold. Create a vision of greatness, happiness and success for yourself. Take the time to envision what you want from life and how your company will help you attain these objectives.

These personal goals should help bring clarity to the questions of why you are in business in the first place and what you want your business to achieve.

However, because these goals are personal, they do not constitute the vision of the company itself. That vision should support your personal goals but must be compelling for your employees. People want to be led by individuals who have a clear idea of what they stand for and where they are going and who act in ways consistent with that vision.

In order to take the long view, you must have the discipline to articulate a vision of what you want your organization to be. Using that vision as a guide, you can determine your long-term goals. Those long-term goals should help you create a series of short-term objectives that can guide your decision-making process and keep you focused on things that will drive your company to achieve the vision you have set.

Size, growth and profitability targets do not constitute a vision for your company. They are not motivating for your employees and will not help you get everyone in the company aligned with your objectives. However, achieving these targets is often the result of performing under a clearly articulated vision. As we will discuss later in this chapter (see page 17), targets for growth and profitability should be integral components of your business plan, and your business plan should support your vision, but the vision must be more important than the numbers themselves. Your vision must help create an ideal that people find compelling and are excited to be part of.

Generally, a vision must aspire to be the very best at something. When you articulate a vision that you would like to be "among the best" or "one of the best," you are not creating objectives that motivate you or your staff. Strive to be the very best at something, so you will continue to shoot for improvement regardless of where you are now. If you try to be "one of the best," you can become good. If you try to become "the best," you can be great.

You may never actually achieve what you set out in your vision, but it will help you make decisions that will drive your business in the direction you desire. In the words of Michel de Montaigne, an important philosopher of the French Renaissance, "Ideals are like the stars to the ancient mariners. We can never reach them, but we guide our path by them."

Long-Term Goals

Once you have written your personal vision and the vision of what you want your company to stand for, it is possible to set some long-term goals for the company.

- What will the company look like in five years if you are on track towards achieving the vision you have set?
- How large will it be?
- What specialty areas will you excel in?
- What clients will you be working for?
- What type of people will be working for you?
- How will the marketplace perceive the company?
- How will employees feel about working at the company?

Once again, it is important to write your answers in order to help you focus. Get a clear picture in your mind of what you want the company to achieve during this period.

This picture of the company in five years should be juxtaposed against your current reality. You should examine where you are today against that five-year plan in terms of your vision, your client base, your size, your employees, your specialty areas and the perception in the marketplace about your organization.

In order to get an accurate reading of your current situation, you must take a critical look at your organization. This is typically done through a Strengths, Weaknesses, Opportunities and Threats (SWOT) analysis. Since you may be too close to the situation, you should not do this exercise alone. You should involve other senior members of your organization and bring in an outside facilitator who can view your situation more objectively and challenge the assumptions you are making.

Once you have a clear picture of where you are today and where you want to go, you can begin to draw a map that will guide you to achieve your long-term objectives. In other words, you can develop short-term goals that will move you along the path to the future you desire.

For example, if your long-term plans call for you to have a successor in place in five years:

- What steps should you be taking in the next six to 18 months that will help you achieve that objective?
- Are there individuals currently on staff who might be groomed to become the successor? If so, what training and development should you undertake immediately to begin the growth process?
- If there is no one on staff who can take on the role, what steps should you take today that will help you identify and attract someone outside your organization who can ultimately fill the role?
- If a long-term objective for the company is to double the size of the average account over the next five years, how will you go about achieving this? Do you have to begin making changes to your creative or budgeting processes, the types of clients you pursue or the type of services you provide?

When evaluating your long-term objectives, you must have specific plans in place that will move you towards those goals over time. The types of changes you desire will not happen overnight. You should look at your business like a farmer looks at his. If the desired result is a healthy crop, the farmer will plant the seeds today, and then water them, feed them, prune them and nurture them to get the best results at the proper time. Farmers have learned that you can't plant the seeds on Tuesday and reap the rewards on Friday.

Business Plans

Many companies do not have business plans, or even budgets, to guide them. If business is healthy, they frequently don't see a need to spend the time to develop a plan.

"Business is great, so why should I bother? I've never done one and look at how successful we've been!"

On the surface, this argument seems compelling. Why should you spend time on something if you have achieved success without it? If your criterion for success is financial performance and you are growing and profitable, why rock the boat?

There are several things to consider.

Is financial performance the only criterion you have to gauge your success? Are there other things you want to achieve personally and professionally? If there are, the planning process will help you accomplish these other objectives as well.

Even if financial performance is your prime motivator, and even if your company is performing well, it is likely that you can achieve faster growth and higher profits if you take the time to develop a plan and use it as a guide to monitor your progress.

If you have completed the vision for yourself and your company, you have already started the business planning process because you have a sense of what you are hoping to achieve in the long run and what criteria you will use to determine whether you are successful.

The value of a business plan lies primarily in the process itself. During this exercise, you will focus considerable time and attention researching and thinking about your business systematically. Thinking about the business is something we typically do not have time to do during the average work week because we are too busy responding to the issues of the day rather than planning for the future.

A proper business plan should take several weeks to prepare and should be done at least annually before the start of the new fiscal year. It should include several narratives that explore critical business issues and several financial reports to be used as benchmarks for the coming year.

The first section of the business plan is the executive summary, which is generally written last, after all other sections have been completed. This is a concisely written document of one to two pages that provides the highlights of the information contained in the plan. These highlights give readers a clear overview of what the plan covers and should make it easier for them to understand how each forthcoming section fits into the overall plan.

Following the executive summary is a section describing the company including the following items:

- **Mission statement:** Driven by the vision you completed earlier; the overall reason why the company is in existence
- **Business definition:** Descriptions of what business you are in, what you perceive as the future of your industry and how your company will compete in that environment
- **Target markets:** Brief overview of your target markets

- **Company history:** Years in business; discussion of past successes, failures and learnings; revenue and profit history
- **Strengths and core competencies:** Descriptions of where the company excels and the areas that are ripe for exploitation
- **Significant challenges:** Descriptions of areas that are obstacles to achieving internal and external success and identification of plans in place to address these challenges
- **Long-term direction:** Overview of your company's long-term direction and analysis of how the current year's plan will lead to that vision

As you have no doubt noticed, some of the items we discussed earlier will help in the development of this section. The mission statement has a direct correlation to the corporate vision. In addition, the SWOT analysis should help define the sections on "business definition," "strengths and core competencies" and "significant challenges."

The next section is a detailed description of the products and services your company produces. You should address the key differentiators you provide in comparison to your competition.

- What areas make your services more appealing to the target audiences?
- In what ways are you trailing your competition in terms of offerings?

You should include a description of any new products or services you plan to introduce in the coming year, especially those that will require an investment of time or capital.

To do a thorough job in this section, you must spend time researching and exploring the industry, your competition and your potential targets. You should try to determine what share of market you have within your specific specialty areas and what share of market you are trying to achieve. To do that, you need to know the size of the overall market and the expectations for growth in the future.

Next, you will want to address your marketing plan. This should be an in-depth examination of your industry and competitors and your plans to market the company in a way that will help set you apart from the competition. Once again, you will need to do some research and give considerable thought to what marketing messages and methods will most resonate with your target audiences and how your marketing efforts will be perceived in comparison to your competitors.

Your marketing strategy should address your plans in networking, speaking opportunities, thought leadership articles, advertising, promotion, social media and other areas that will allow you to generate increased awareness of the company and some of its leaders. You will find some helpful ideas on how to maximize your marketing success in the section entitled "Getting and Keeping the Business" on page 21.

Address the inner workings of your company and thoroughly examine how it is managed and organized. This section should explore issues related to items such as staffing, management and pricing.

- What are the fundamental characteristics of the internal functions of the organization?
- What significant issues must be addressed to improve the odds of success in the future?

In professional service organizations, the greatest risk generally comes from not having the right employees in place in key roles within the company. This risk can take many forms. For example, there may not be an adequate succession plan to replace the principal or other senior personnel within the organization. In addition, there may be one or more important client relationships that are tied to specific individuals, increasing the risk of losing the client if you lose the employee.

To complete this section of the business plan adequately, you should examine the consequences to the company if any individual were to leave unexpectedly. If the consequences would be dire, you need to consider ways to reduce this risk and include these ideas in your plan. In addition, you should consider if there are areas of the company where you need to upgrade performance through training or replacement of individuals who are underperforming.

This section should also explore how the company is managed on a day-to-day basis.

- Which groups are empowered to make specific decisions?
- What does an organizational chart look like for the company?
- Are reporting relationships clear to all members of the staff?

If there are problems in any of these areas, you should include plans to address these issues.

Finally, this section should examine what systems and processes are working well and which ones should be modified or replaced to help the company achieve its goals. This might include computer equipment or services; software and systems for accounting, time reporting and billing; client contract terms; billing rates; and client profit-and-loss management.

Before you can accurately assess the financial projections for the coming year, you need to analyze the financial history of the company. First, review the financial statements for the company for the past three to five years.

- What type of growth and profitability have you been able to achieve?
- How has your compensation-to-income ratio changed during that time?
- What are the percentages of other operating expenses compared to revenue, and how do they compare to industry standards?
- If certain expense categories are not in line with industry averages, are there steps you can take in the new year that should be incorporated into your plan?

You must also analyze the details in two critical areas: client income and employee compensation. You should review the changes in income for each client, comparing the current year to the previous year to determine which clients appear to have the best opportunity for growth in the upcoming year. For employees, you should compare the compensation for each person to acceptable industry standards to make certain you are adequately compensating your star employees and not overpaying marginal players. This plan will help develop the budget for the new year.

Once you have thoroughly examined and understand the implications of your financial history, you are prepared to develop a budget for the upcoming year. It is generally best to develop the annual budget by looking at expected performance for each month. While some items, such as rent and utilities, can reasonably be expected to remain constant from month to month, others may fluctuate. Specifically, income may rise and fall depending on items such as anticipated projects, the number of billable days each month, new business and lost clients. Compensation may fluctuate as well if you budget for raises at specific times or plan to hire new employees as the year progresses. The advantage of budgeting on a monthly basis is that you can compare actual results to what you anticipated as the year progresses.

Obviously, your budget must include any expenditures required to execute the critical initiatives you have outlined in the narrative portion of the business plan. With the help of your accountant or financial person, you should also develop a projected cash flow and year-end balance sheet.

Another significant use of the budget is to monitor and plan for areas where you feel you should improve your performance year over year. By comparing your upcoming budget to the actual performance from the previous year, you can see where critical ratios are improving or deteriorating. Although it can be highly speculative, many companies find it helpful to include a three- to four-year projection in their business plan. This method allows you to start building towards the long-term goals you've outlined previously.

If you need further information on the development of tools related to preparing a business plan or for managing your business on an ongoing basis, you can find detailed information in the section entitled "Building and Maintaining Profitability" on page 67.

Managing Your Time

Once you've defined your vision and used it to determine your long-term goals and to develop your business plans, you must bring them to life. Every day you will be faced with issues and problems that seem to absorb every waking hour. It's easy to get caught up in the exigency of the day and lose sight of the long-term picture.

My company is Second Quadrant Solutions. The name was derived from the Time Management Matrix introduced by Stephen Covey, author of *The 7 Habits of Highly Effective People*. The basic concept of the matrix is that everything you can do is either important or unimportant and either urgent or not urgent. Therefore, everything falls into one of four categories, as seen on page 20.

How you spend your time will determine how effective you are. Obviously, activities in the first quadrant must be done first because they are both urgent and important. However, if you spend most of your time here, there can be significant consequences.

Quadrant III activities are very seductive, especially today. The phone rings, we answer it. An e-mail comes through, we read and respond. Text messages, slack and instant messages constantly bombard us and, with the prevalence of open offices, interruptions are seemingly endless.

	Urgent	Not Urgent
	Quadrant I— **Necessity**	**Quadrant II—** **Effectiveness**
Important	Crises Pressing problems Deadline-driven projects, meetings, reports	Preparation/Planning Prevention Relationships
	Quadrant III— **Deception**	**Quadrant IV—** **Waste and Excess**
Not **Important**	Needless interruptions Unnecessary reports Unimportant meetings, calls, e-mail	Busywork Time wasters Excessive TV, social media

The problem with these activities is that, although they're urgent, we can't tell if they're important until we see what they're about. If they are legitimately Quadrant I activities, you need to address them. However, if you can identify them as Quadrant III, they are, by definition, *not* important and therefore should not take your time away from important items in Quadrants I and II.

Quadrant II activities, because they are not urgent, are easy to put off until tomorrow. However, they are the most important things you can do to be effective, and they are the only activities that result in a positive frame of mind. Importantly, as you spend more time on Quadrant II activities, you will reduce the number of urgencies that arise.

Getting and
Keeping the Business

*If people like you, they'll listen to you, but if
they trust you, they'll do business with you.*

—Zig Ziglar

An essential aspect of building a successful business is your ability to sustain enough revenue to attract and retain talent, invest in new strategic initiatives and achieve the goals you have defined for yourself. Business growth is dependent on how successful you are in several areas, such as developing trusted relationships, marketing your company, delivering excellent results to clients, identifying opportunities to grow client engagements and staying aware of how satisfied your clients are with your service.

Very often, companies make the mistake of spending too large a percentage of their time on only one or two of these areas and largely ignore the others. For example, it is very seductive to focus most of your attention on delivering quality work on existing business. Although this is a critical component in the process, no single tactic should be executed to the exclusion of the others.

This chapter will explore each of these topics in detail and will hopefully illuminate why they are vital to the success of your business.

Developing Trusted Relationships

In the grand scheme, virtually everything you have accomplished in life up to this point, and everything else you can expect in the future, was done with the help of other people. When people are dealing with an issue, their first action generally is to reach out to people they know and trust who can help them in some way.

For example, if you are looking for a job, you would probably contact many of your acquaintances to see if they know of any opportunities or if they can connect you with others who might be looking to hire someone. Conversely, if you are trying to find new employees to hire, you would reach out to people you know for leads.

In other words, in terms of the job market, most people on both ends of the search use their personal contacts to solve their problem. When an important decision like hiring takes place, people generally go to other people they trust and look for help and guidance.

This concept extends to many other aspects of life, such as when you are trying to find a doctor or a dentist, when you are considering what neighborhood you should move to, when you are contemplating what restaurant to eat at or which movie to see or when you are wondering which brand of electronics to buy. In these situations, you are likely to search out people you know and trust and ask their advice and direction.

It stands to reason, therefore, that the more people you have in your circle of trusted relationships, the better able you will be to find success through those relationships. Spending time developing and maintaining these relationships is critical and must become a regular part of your daily routine.

While there are significant rewards to be gained if you have attracted many people you can trust and can count on, this process cannot work unless you first become a trusted friend to each of them. You cannot expect to make withdrawals from someone's emotional bank account until you have made repeated deposits that provide you with enough equity in the relationship to "take something out."

In other words, the real challenge is to develop relationships by providing value to as many people as you can, over and over again. You can do this by sharing information, resources or connections to others who might help. By giving of yourself and helping many others, you are building the types of relationships that may have benefits for you in the future, either directly or indirectly.

According to Jeffrey Gitomer, a well-known expert on networking, the adage "It's not what you know but who you know" should be modified. It's not "who you know" but "who knows you" that really matters. The goal is to develop an outstanding reputation in your field and to generate "buzz" about yourself and your company.

By taking the time to assist others every chance you get, you will develop the type of reputation that should generate positive discussions about you, even when you are not present. The more positive experiences people have with you, the more likely that your name and accomplishments will be discussed when one of them meets someone else. If the second person has positive feelings about you as well, the conversation will enhance and reinforce the feelings of both individuals.

Let's examine how this situation might lead to business. Imagine that you have two acquaintances (Bill and Susan) who think you are terrific. They may or may not know each other, but they may know many of the same people. Let's assume that one of their mutual friends (Beth) needs the type of service you provide. Beth asks two of her trusted friends (Bill and Susan) for help, and they both recommend you. With endorsements from two (or more) trusted friends, it is likely that she will contact you.

This scenario may seem unlikely, but there are numerous examples every day where this situation plays out and leads to positive results. For example, I recall one company owner who contacted me because she was having difficulty managing her business successfully. When we met, she told me that for the past six months she had told everyone she trusted in the business about her problems, and five of them had told her, "You really need to meet with Darryl Salerno!"

I do not know who four of the five people were, but she became a client of mine before our first meeting. She was determined to hire me before we even met because I had received the unsolicited endorsement of people she trusted.

The reason many people fall short in their endeavor to develop these results is that the process is initially a slow build, and they frequently quit too early to reap the rewards. It takes time to develop the quality and quantity of relationships that can create the buzz you desire, but the mathematics of networking are extremely compelling and can reach dizzying heights with proper diligence and persistence.

If you only know two people, and if those two people meet each other, only one conversation can take place that might include a discussion about you. If you know a third person, three conversations could take place; a fourth person would lead to six conversations; and a fifth to 10. With each new person you meet, you add potential new conversations equal to the number of people you already know.

While these numbers may be interesting, they are probably too small to produce any significant results, but what happens as the number of people in your network increases? The chart below shows just how rapidly the number of connections can grow as you add to your base of contacts.

People you know	Possible connections
2	1
5	10
10	45
50	1,225
100	4,950
200	20,100
500	125,250
1,000	500,500
2,000	2,000,100

As you can see, the number of connections explodes as your circle increases rather modestly. For example, adding 300 more people to your network (from 200 to 500) increases the connections between them by a factor of six, adding more than 100,000 new connections.

The chart on page 25 above indicates the number of potential connections among the people you know *if they know each other.* While it is possible there will be many instances where people you know also know one another, that is not the most powerful aspect of networking. Far more compelling is the fact that every person you know also knows many more people you have not yet met, and any one of them could be someone you may need to accomplish your goals.

To put it into perspective, if everyone had a network of only 200 people, you would be one step removed from up to 40,000 people and two steps removed from as many as 8,000,000 people. This means that if you asked the 200 people you know for help, they could each ask their 200 acquaintances and the request would be shared with up to 40,000 individuals with little effort.

Since it is clear you will need other individuals to help you achieve your goals, it stands to reason that if you can build a strong, large network of people who would be eager to help you, you will achieve success far more easily. So, the question is, "How do I do it effectively?"

As discussed previously (see page 23), in order to have people eager to help you, you must first make significant deposits into their emotional bank accounts and find ways to help *them.* You should look at every encounter with another person as an opportunity to do something to help them.

In order to determine how you can help someone, you must develop and hone exceptional listening skills. You need to ask questions about what troubles them. You should probe deep into these areas to discover the real pain points. You also need to pay attention to body language and tone of voice, which will frequently contradict the words being spoken.

In many instances, people will tell you what they think you want to hear, such as "Things are great!" or "Everything is terrific!" If you listen to tone of voice and watch facial expressions and body language, you may discover that there are unspoken issues where you can help.

Once you are certain that you understand the problem facing the person, you can provide some guidance that will help alleviate it. You may have an idea of how they might deal with the situation or can recommend a book or website that might provide some assistance.

Most importantly, maybe there is someone in your network who can help, and you can suggest making the connection. If one of the best ways to provide help is to connect one person to another, it stands to reason that the larger your network is, the more valuable you are to everyone in your network. You will find that if you are well connected and eager to help others, many people will reach out to you for assistance. Every time someone does, you have an easy opportunity to make an investment in her emotional bank account, strengthening your network with very little proactive effort.

Building a network requires persistence. Because it rarely pays immediate dividends, it is very easy to justify spending time on other activities that are more pressing. This is a mistake. You must consistently invest time every week in this area in order to reap potentially enormous rewards. If you have discipline and continue to spend time each week, in the future you will have fewer pressing issues to deal with because you will have a much fuller pipeline for new clients, new potential employees and people to help you.

Many people are at a loss regarding how to begin this process and make it successful. It really is quite simple. Go to places where you can meet people, engage them in conversations about themselves and their challenges, make a connection to them and follow up after the meeting.

When trying to find places to meet people, many of us think of networking events and feel the pressure of attempting to sell to them there. Networking events are fine, but they are not the best places to meet, and being in the selling mode is clearly the wrong approach. You can meet people at parties, industry events, awards programs, sporting events, your child's soccer games or the doctor's office.

You may actually find yourself more successful at social events. Without the pressure to be in a selling mode, you are likely to engage someone in a more genuine conversation and have a much better chance to learn about them and their issues.

You are also more likely to make a connection. You may discover that you went to the same school, grew up in the same neighborhood, go to the same doctor and know some of the same people. Each of these things will help you make a connection with the other person and enhance your ability to become a friend rather than a potential vendor.

After meeting people, it's a good idea to follow up with them to strengthen the connection, recap some of the things you discussed and provide some thoughts on their most pressing issues. If you have listened carefully during your original encounter, you may have learned of some major upcoming event in their life. Contacting the person again after that major event is a smart idea, just to check in to see how it went.

If you like the person and want to maintain a relationship, you will want to reach out periodically. After each contact with someone, you should make a note on your calendar or tag the e-mail exchange with the time to reach out again.

Periodically reach out to each person in your network, even if it's just to say hello and see how they are doing. If you haven't seen someone in a while, invite her for a cup of coffee or lunch. In every conversation, listen for upcoming events and other opportunities to reach out again.

Challenge yourself to continually work on building your network. Add 10 new contacts on LinkedIn each week. Call three to five people you know each week to check in with them and strengthen your connection. Each week, reach out to one or two people you've never met but have common connections with and, in every case, listen for opportunities to help them with their issues.

Marketing Your Company

Networking is a smart way to get people to know you and your company personally. It will enhance your ability to build your  business because you will develop the types of trusted relationships that people look for when awarding work.

However, networking alone cannot give you the results you desire. There is a limit to how many people you can meet and maintain strong relationships with. You must also make the effort to market your agency more broadly.

Many companies are aware of the need to market their firms and spend a good deal of time and money to build brand awareness. Ironically, the communications companies frequently do the worst job in marketing themselves, although it is their primary product when selling to clients.

I have worked with many public relations agencies over the years that do an excellent job on their clients' communications needs and an abysmal job on their own. They get so bogged down on client work that they forget the most important client: their own company.

The best agencies understand the importance of handling communications correctly. They assign agency marketing to a strong internal team and make them realize that they are working on the most important client: the agency. They budget the time to execute this process, develop a communications plan for the year, provide regular updates to management regarding progress and take advantage of opportunities that arise serendipitously during the year, just as they would for any client program.

In short, they do not put their own marketing on hold for the sake of other client programs any more than they would put one client's program on hold for the sake of another.

When considering marketing your agency, you should strive to tell the outside world about all the wonderful things you are doing and the successes you are having. You need to announce when you win new clients, make significant hires, add new services, develop new concepts and speak at industry events. Every agency experiences many positive developments. It is important that you put in the effort to make the rest of the world aware of how you are doing.

One area you should not overlook is awards submissions. Many industry awards are highly regarded and can enhance the reputation of agencies that are nominated for, or win, awards. When you have programs you are proud of, you need to take the time to submit those programs into multiple awards programs. The more frequently your agency is highlighted as a finalist, or wins the award, the more credibility you receive in the area the award covers.

If the industry perceives your agency as "hot," it will be easier to attract new clients and new employees. Everyone wants to work with a winner.

I know that this is just common sense, but common sense is not always common practice. Do not let your marketing activities lapse because of other pressures. You would not let your clients do that. Don't let your agency do it either.

Delivering Quality Work

The key to providifng excellent work for your clients starts with hiring and growing superior employees. We will deal with this process in the section entitled "Getting and Keeping Employees" on page 43. While this is the starting point, it is also critical that you develop the necessary processes to allow you to create creative and strategic programs.

Without excellent programs, even the best employees will be unable to provide quality service. With proper attention to the development of the program, your superior staff can produce results that will delight your clients and win recognition for value-added performance.

The first step in creating a great program is a disciplined brainstorming process, which allows for the creation of a plentitude of potential ideas that can be explored to bring the client's program to life. While this may seem self-evident, you may be surprised at how many agencies do not pursue brainstorming in the proper way.

Often, once a good idea is proposed during the brainstorming process, the group begins to dig deep into that idea, fleshing out the ways in which it can be implemented. This is more like a programming exercise than a brainstorming session and will limit the number of ideas that can be explored. The purpose of brainstorming is to produce as many potential ideas as possible. After all, the best idea might be the 87th one to come up. If you short circuit the brainstorm by exploring one of the early ideas, you may never get to the best idea.

Proper brainstorming requires a structured approach to achieve the types of results you desire for extraordinary client programs. As a result, the best agencies have taken the time to train several facilitators who are used as the leaders of all brainstorming sessions. I strongly suggest that you consider taking this course of action for your agency and provide formal training in this area. As a starting point, let me review some of the primary things to consider when running a brainstorming session.

First, the facilitator of a session needs to remain objective. Therefore, no one should facilitate a session for a problem they "own." In other words, the person who is running the account, or the new business pitch, should never facilitate the session. They are the sponsor of the session and should participate in it but not be the one to run it.

Additionally, the facilitator is not there to contribute ideas. They are there to manage the process, fight negativity and keep the session flowing productively. We will identify the process shortly, but first we will explore the effect of negativity on the brainstorming process.

The most debilitating thing for a brainstorming session is to allow negative thoughts and comments to derail the process. Once you allow negatives into the discussion, you will find that many people will not contribute ideas as readily because they are fearful that their contribution will be rejected. The fundamental rule of all brainstorming sessions is that there are "no negatives." Every idea, even if said in jest, should be accepted and recorded. Very often, ideas that seem ridiculous on the surface are catalysts for other ideas that are real winners.

Many statements can effectively kill the ideation process. Some of the more common ones are:

- "It's too expensive."
- "That's not the way they/we do things."

- "It'll never work."
- "We tried that already."
- "They'll never buy it."

The facilitator is responsible to make certain that these types of negative statements do not find their way into the session. They must also be alert to more subtle comments that can lead to negativity. Participants will often try to sound cooperative, starting statements with:

- "I'm just playing devil's advocate."
- "I know we're not supposed to be negative, but …"
- "I just want to clarify what's possible."

Just like the more obvious examples above, these types of comments must be stopped immediately.

Participants will also make negative comments about the idea they are about to share with the group, saying:

- "I doubt this could work, but …"
- "This will probably be [too expensive, risky, boring], but …"

At the start, the facilitator should set the ground rules for the session in writing and post these rules, so they are visible throughout the session. When faced with any negative comments, whether directed at someone else's ideas or one's own, the facilitator must address the negativity immediately and put a stop to it.

The goal of the facilitator is to help uncover as many ideas as possible and foster a spirit of contribution. They should encourage participation and reinforce the efforts of people who are engaged in the process. If you are facilitating, you should listen very carefully, write down every idea exactly as it was uttered and orally repeat the ideas as you write them. Don't exclude ideas that are silly or said in a joking manner. If an idea is repeated from earlier in the session, write it down the second time as well. The objective is to keep people generating ideas. Any editing you do will hamper that creative process.

To foster maximum participation, you should encourage people as much as possible. Compliment them for their ideas, especially the risky ones. Make certain you also provide reinforcing nonverbal feedback by smiling, applauding, showing interest and moving closer to participants.

Once you are asked to facilitate a session, you should arrange to meet with the person who is ultimately responsible for the outcome: the sponsor. Agree on the single problem you want to resolve in the brainstorming session. The problem should be simple to understand but provocative and significant. At this same meeting, you should discuss the criteria that the final solution must meet, such as budget restrictions, timing, tonality and measurement/results.

You should also encourage the sponsor to develop a creative brief to be distributed to the brainstorming participants in advance. The brief should cover the current market conditions faced by the client, an understanding of the perceptions about the client/product in the marketplace and what changes you hope to make in those perceptions through this program, a description of the audiences and influencers you are trying to affect and a definition of the problem you are trying to address.

The final preparation for the brainstorming process is to decide who should be invited. Optimally, you should have between five and eight participants, each of whom is invited for a purpose. You should be careful not to include more than two or three people who have knowledge of the problem. In order to generate exciting new ideas, most of the attendees should be new to the client and the problem. You should also strive to include as much diversity as possible, including different ages, genders, styles, backgrounds, functions and job levels.

Once the session has started, it should cover the following elements, in order:

- Explanation of the situation

- Definition of the problem
- Description of the criteria
- Brainstorming/ideation process
- Idea selection
- Review of next steps

To review the situation, have the sponsor spend a few minutes providing the background on the problem, focusing attention on how the client/product fits into the current marketplace, what issues are suspected of causing the current situation, what audiences you are trying to influence and what attitudes or behaviors you are trying to shift. During this process, all participants, including the facilitator, are encouraged to ask questions so everyone truly understands the background as well as possible.

Following the situation review, you should move to a definition of the specific problem you are trying to address during the session. The facilitator should write "How to" on the flip chart and allow the sponsor to complete the phrase. Optimally, the problem statement should include a sense of conflict. This will allow for a more focused ideation session.

The final step before the ideation process is to have the sponsor describe the criteria that the final proposal will have to meet including financial limitations/budget, timing, tone and required results. The facilitator should record these criteria on the flip chart, and then post them on the wall and cover them. It is important to describe the criteria in advance of the session so you can use them later as a litmus test for the ideas you create, but you do not want the potential limitations to be considered during the ideation process, so you need to make certain they are not visible for the next phase.

When the ideation process begins, there are several rules that must be followed. The facilitator should list these rules at the start of the exercise and post them on the wall, so they are visible throughout the session. The rules are simple and straightforward: use no negatives, choose quantity over quality, build off the ideas of others, agree that everyone's equal and have fun!

We have already discussed the issues around allowing negative thoughts and comments to enter the process. At this point, you should reinforce the concept that there are no bad ideas and you are trying to explore all options. Although it is difficult to suspend judgment during this exercise, assure the participants that there will be time to evaluate all the ideas later in the session, but, since we are striving to produce as many ideas as possible, anything that will constrict the flow of new concepts must be eliminated at this point.

Brainstorming has been shown to be much more successful in creating new ideas than having the same people work on the problem individually. This is true because ideas from one person generally trigger ideas in others. For this reason, the facilitator should encourage people to build on the ideas of other participants. This means having people consider other concepts that are related in some way to the ones being discussed. It does not mean they should begin working through the details or implementation of an idea. That process will take place during the programming phase.

For example, if you are trying to reach athletic males in their 20s and someone suggests that you develop a surfing event at the beach, do not allow the conversation to drift towards details like who should be invited, what beach should be considered and how to reach potential audiences. Instead, encourage people to think of other events that might appeal to this audience or other things to consider doing on a beach.

Enforcing the "everyone's equal" rule is very important. Frequently, the most senior people in the group will dominate the discussion and intimidate their junior counterparts or those who have less experience. Anything that detracts from abundant ideation must be avoided. As the facilitator, be careful not to defer to senior individuals, and make certain to recognize the contributions of the junior participants so they will be more inclined to participate.

Finally, the most productive brainstorming sessions are fun. People are more creative and prolific when they are enjoying themselves. Whenever possible, encourage humor.

As you lead the ideation process, keep your energy level high. Applaud every idea. Encourage participation. Keep the ideas flowing by asking questions during lulls:

- "What are some things we can do?"
- "What else?"
- "What would solve this problem?"
- "What's the craziest thing we can do?"
- "How can we build off that idea?"
- "How else can we [insert the stated problem]?"
- "What kind of contests could we run?"
- "What events would make sense?"
- "If you were the audience, what would appeal to you?"

As you proceed through the process, you can encourage more participation in an area by asking, "What else?" When you want to close down a particular line of thinking, say "Anything else?" Very subtly, this will imply that it is time to move on to the next area of ideation.

Once you have reached the end of the ideation process, you will enter the next phase of the meeting. Hopefully, you will have created a wide variety of potential program ideas, and it is time to select the concepts that have the greatest appeal and potential.

There are many ways you can winnow the list to make it manageable, but the objective is to involve the brainstorming participants in the process as much as possible. One method is to give each participant 10 stickers and allow them to place the stickers next to the ideas they like the best. They can put all of them on a single idea, put one sticker on each of their 10 favorites or anything in between. This method allows people to weight their voting based on the strength of their commitment to a concept.

Another method is to have each person write down her three favorite ideas, rotate around the room and check off the ideas as they are identified. In either case, the three to four ideas that get the most votes are the ones that should be considered for exploration.

At this point, you should reveal the criteria you developed at the start of the meeting and check the chosen ideas to make certain they can be developed in a way that will satisfy the needs as they were identified.

Finally, you need to work with the group to determine the next steps to develop the selected programs.

- Which members of the team will take responsibility to expand the selected concepts?
- When will the documents be ready for review?
- Who will make the final decision on what to present to the client?

When done properly, a creative brainstorming session has the potential to help you generate ideas that will better solve the client's problem. However, it is only one part of a structured approach to win business and provide excellent work. Equally important is the way the program is designed and presented.

Programming

All communications programs are created to enhance the overall business objectives of the client. Without that focus, most programs become nothing more than a series of tactics that are not necessarily improving the client's business.

When constructing a proposal, you should track against a specific model that will lead your thinking and tell the right story to the client. Your programming should follow a specific outline that tracks against the client's situation and fulfills the business objectives of the company.

- Situation
- Business objectives
- Communications objectives
- Strategy
- Tactics
- Anticipated results

As you build the program, make certain that each element you list for a category is addressed in subsequent categories. In other words, you should have at least one strategy to address each communications objective you've listed. Conversely, there should be no strategies that do not support a communications objective.

Once you have developed your program, the final step in producing a winning pitch is conducting a formal rehearsal. Your rehearsal should be conducted as if it is the actual presentation to the client in real time. In other words, if you are given 90 minutes to present, you should conduct your rehearsal in 90 minutes. In that way, you can assure that you will make all the relevant points clearly and concisely in the time allotted.

The rehearsal should be conducted in front of several people who play the role of the client. These individuals should be drawn from people who are not involved in the program, do not work on the client's business and can play an objective role in the process. They should also be armed with enough background to ask tough questions during and after the presentation. Many times, the pitch is lost because of poor responses to questions rather than the formal presentation. Q&A should be rehearsed as stringently as the presentation itself.

Some people feel that this type of rehearsal is not necessary, but the truth is that the first time you give a presentation is a rehearsal. Do you really want that rehearsal to take place in front of the client?

It is generally a good idea to also run the rehearsal in a very tight time frame. For example, if the client has promised you 90 minutes to present, you should also run through the presentation several times in 15 to 20 minutes. This exercise forces each presenter to focus on the most cogent facts on each slide rather than getting bogged down in the minutiae of the information. In addition, if your actual presentation is truncated for some reason, the presenters will feel comfortable despite the pressure of limited time.

If you will be presenting directly from slides, keep the copy to a minimum. Use few bullets and words and rely on visuals when possible. You don't want your audience to be reading the slides; you want them to pay attention to you. Use the content of each slide as a guide to present your ideas more fully. Only use a large amount of copy when the slides will be sent to the client and more detail is required.

Keeping the Business

Clearly, the most important aspect of building your business is to perform quality, valuable work for your clients, but doing great work goes beyond executing the assignments you have agreed to take on. To truly delight your clients, you must develop a culture where people become fully engaged in the business of your client's business.

Your employees should understand the inner workings of their client's organization and should be well versed on the competitive landscape faced by their clients. By immersing themselves in their client's issues, they can help provide strategic solutions that will lead the client's thinking and become invaluable partners in the process.

Your agency's ability to maintain long-term client relationships and to grow the size of existing accounts is largely determined by your ability to suggest strategic ideas that will make your client contacts heroes in their organizations. Flawless execution is important but expected. It's a commodity that clients feel they can purchase elsewhere—probably for less than they are paying you. The most significant assets that set you apart from your competition are your counsel and ideas. You must always be on the alert to the things that are keeping your clients awake at night and develop program elements that will solve their problems.

Beyond understanding the client's business and competitive framework, you and your employees must develop excellent listening skills. Sensitivity to body language and tone of voice as well as the nonverbal messages you receive is crucial. You must be very good at asking probing, open-ended questions that lead your clients to reveal areas of pain.

When you factor in reduced spending by some clients and the loss of others, most agencies lose 30–35% of their business year to year. To grow by 15%, we must find 50% as much business in one year as we executed as programs the previous year. Even without growth on existing business, keeping each client for an additional year should reduce the loss factor to 20–25% and will greatly accelerate your growth.

Finally, client satisfaction must be solicited and measured, and any hints of dissatisfaction should be addressed quickly and completely. If your client is not completely delighted with your work on their behalf, you are at risk of losing their business to someone else.

You must implement a client satisfaction measurement process. Some agencies send a simple written survey and hope that their clients will take the time to fill in the information and return it. Others use outside consultants to engage clients in a dialogue in order to uncover areas where the client may not be completely satisfied. Regardless of the method you use, you need to respond quickly to the issues raised by the client and implement any warranted changes.

Getting and Keeping Employees

*Always treat your employees exactly as you
want them to treat your best customers.*

—Stephen R. Covey

When I took over the reigns of Creamer Dickson Basford (CDB) (now Havas PR), I did a great deal of soul searching about what I wanted for myself and how the company could help me achieve my personal objectives.

Having been in the business for 20 years at that point, I had been managed by a wide variety of people and had observed the management style of countless others. A few of those managers seemed to have the innate ability to engage the people who worked for them and were extremely effective in getting exceptional compliance with achieving their goals. Under those managers, employees were happy, committed and dedicated and performed better than they did under other managers.

When I was asked to become chief executive officer at CDB, I was determined to create the kind of work environment where people wanted to come each day, where they wanted to learn and succeed and where they wanted to collaborate with their coworkers to accomplish the goals of the company. In short, I wanted to create the best work environment in the industry.

While this desire was for selfish reasons—creating a place where I wanted to work and leaving a legacy I could be proud of—it was clear to me that, if we were successful in this quest, we would have very little voluntary turnover, a deeply committed workforce and an environment that would attract the very best people in the industry. I realized that with the best people, we could do exceptional work on behalf of our clients and make a lot of money at the same time.

In a very short period, we generated significant results. According to The Holmes Report, after our first full year, "The turnaround at Magnet Communications (formerly CDB) has been nothing short of remarkable. The firm, once regarded as a sweatshop, has developed into one of the most progressive workplaces in the industry."

I believe this philosophy should be an objective for every agency. Many studies confirm that people who are happy in their jobs perform better and, if your people feel valued and are given the chance to grow, there is a much better chance they will stay with you. When you consider that the only difference between your agency and the competition is the people who work for you, it is imperative that you do everything you can to retain and develop your best people.

To do this, you need to focus on how you treat people and how your people treat one another. This focus requires a well-balanced, professional development program that teaches all supervisory personnel how to lead and manage their staffs.

Most agency employees enter at junior levels and advance based on how well they perform specific tasks. Many are Type A personalities who strive for perfection. As they grow in their positions, they tend to look for recognition in the things they do themselves; they learn to trust their own capabilities.

At one point, they are promoted and placed in a role where they need to manage a team. This situation puts them in an entirely different position. They will no longer be judged by what they can do themselves but by how well they can get others to perform.

In many cases, without proper training, new supervisors continue to do much of the work they were doing before. They are reluctant to delegate because they only trust how well they can execute something and are often unwilling to put their career in the hands of people below them.

You will frequently hear these types of managers say things like:
- "I can do it better myself."
- "It will take too much time to explain what I want."
- "I can do it faster."
- "I don't want to overburden my staff."
- "This is so important that I can't trust anyone else to do it."

There is an element of truth to most of these feelings, but this mindset leads to a stagnant organization because people are not given a chance to learn new skills. The employees below the supervisor are not given an opportunity to advance, and the supervisor is not able to reduce her workload to take on new responsibilities. There are also significant financial consequences that we will address (see the section entitled "Overservicing" on page 69).

Let's examine how this scenario should work for the advancement of the agency. When an assignment comes in, there is a tendency in any organization to have it handled as efficiently as possible, so it is given to the person who handles that type of work best. This method allows the task to be completed most rapidly. It is a focus on rapid production.

While speed is important, it is less important than the development of the people in the agency. Rather than using the person to complete the task rapidly, why not use the task to develop another person to become an expert in that area? If done correctly, your organization can become stronger because you now have multiple people who can handle that type of assignment. In addition, the skills of your staff continue to grow and improve. Instead of focusing on production, you are focusing on increasing your production capability and capacity.

In the words of Agha Hasan Abedi, renowned banker and philanthropist, "The conventional wisdom of management is getting work done through people, but real management is developing people through work." In other words, when you are considering an assignment, the first thing you should think of is, "Who needs to learn how to do this?" This process will be addressed more fully (see the section entitled "Delegation" on page 60).

Over the course of my career, I have come across many managers whom I consider to be "Bosses of Mass Destruction." These are individuals who run their organizations or groups with little regard to the effect their style will have on the people who work for them.

It's important to avoid many of the pitfalls that these managers fall prey to. The rest of this chapter is designed to provide guidance in critical areas of excellent management techniques.

Leadership

There is a huge difference between being a manager and being a leader. You are a manager because someone appointed you to a position where you hold sway over others. You can, of course, use that position to dictate what you want those people to do. They will do it because they were told to do it—whether or not they really want to. That situation can frequently lead to resentment and discord in the organization.

Leadership, on the other hand, allows you to get people to willingly do what you want them to do. Some people seem to be natural leaders. You can frequently find leaders at any level or at any age. However, leadership can be learned and improved.

To lead people, you need to be positive and upbeat. You need to see a future that is better than the present. You need an exciting vision of what is possible. That's inspirational. If I believe you can lead me to a better tomorrow, I am more willing to follow you there.

You must set high goals for the group to aspire to. This allows them to understand what they are striving to achieve and helps tie everyone's goals together. If they all believe in what you are trying to attain, they will gladly do the things you've asked of them.

In addition, great leaders are advocates for the people who work for them. They take the blame when things go wrong and share the credit when things go right.

Motivation

Motivation is an important component in managing personnel. However, motivating someone is not really possible. Motivation is internally driven. People are motivated by the things that are important to them. You can't motivate them, but you need them motivated.

Great managers change their style to connect with each person working for them in a way that will resonate best with the employee. The secret is to uncover what motivates each person and tie that to what you want to achieve. Don't assume you know what motivates someone. People are motivated by promotions, recognition, money, trust, responsibility, respect, challenge, or any number of other things.

The goal is to get to know each employee well enough to understand what gets her excited and what will make her perform with enthusiasm. Once you understand these things, your job is to determine how you can tap into what motivates her and show how the assignment you are proposing will help her achieve her goals.

You can certainly ask the employee what things she finds interesting or exciting, but you may not always get an answer that's clear. Often, people can't articulate what they want, but "they'll know it when they see it." You need to pay attention to tone of voice and body language to identify when she appears particularly excited or interested.

Every person is motivated by something. When someone appears unmotivated, it is a sign that she is not motivated by what she is doing. It does not mean that nothing will motivate her. It means that she is not currently involved in something she finds motivating.

Handling Praise, Criticism and Conflict

Praise

In the course of a day, many things will go right, and some things will go wrong. To keep your staff engaged and striving to produce excellent work, it's important to give praise and criticism correctly.

A good leader will share credit when things are successful. It's important to know when to provide praise to those who did a good job.

First and foremost, when you feel something is praiseworthy, you should try to provide that encouragement as soon as possible after the task is complete. Waiting for a performance review, or some other convenient moment, diminishes the positive feelings that the employee will have and reduces the effectiveness of using the praise to reinforce excellent behavior and success.

Praising someone is not just saying, "Hey, good job!" The purpose of giving praise is to provide the employee with the sense of what types of performance are most important to the company and to the continued growth of the employee. Therefore, you need to be specific about what you are praising. You are commending the person on some specific action she took to encourage more of the same in the future.

While providing praise is very important, make sure you don't overdo it. When you exaggerate the magnitude of what was done or give praise too frequently, you diminish the effectiveness of the process and make the praise meaningless.

So how do you give praise? There are several ways to tell an employee that you value the work she's just completed, and different methods work better with different people.

In some cases, you may want to send a note or an e-mail and copy more senior people in the organization. This action shows that you are giving credit and are being an advocate for your employee. It works particularly well with employees who are interested in promotions, salary increases and recognition.

In other cases, you may want to celebrate these successes more broadly by announcing them at staff meetings or awarding the employee with some type of honor given on a regular basis. Many people enjoy this recognition. However, some do not want to be recognized in public. You need to understand the person well enough to know what will work and what won't.

In any case, I strongly urge you to visit the employee's workspace, talk to her one on one privately and tell her about the job she did. You can always follow up with one of the recommendations above, but the face-to-face discussion should be done regardless.

Criticism

The word "criticism" has a negative connotation. Most people use this word to mean "finding fault and disapproval." As a result, many people are loath to provide it regularly and, when they do, it comes across harshly.

When something goes wrong, the purpose of criticism is to try to ensure that the behavior is not repeated. Criticism should be designed to help the employee become more proficient and better at her job. The goal is to provide criticism in a way that she will be open to hearing it and open to change, so there are certain things you should keep in mind to be most effective.

Just like with praise, criticism should be specific, identifying a particular action but not attacking the individual. It should also be done as soon as possible after the incident.

However, unlike praise, criticism should *always* be done in private. Nothing is gained by criticizing someone in public. When you do, the general result is that the person becomes embarrassed, and her inner voice is focused on that embarrassment and anger towards the criticizer. She is less likely to accept responsibility for the problem and therefore more likely to repeat the problem later.

There are subtle ways to approach critiquing someone's performance to get the best long-term results. Generally, when there is a mistake, managers focus their attention, and the conversation, on the mistake. Often, the employee feels attacked and defends the fact that there were other factors that contributed to the problem. While this defense is frequently true, it stops the employee from embracing how she added to the issue. This approach decreases the probability of the employee learning from the error and taking actions to avoid it in the future.

Rather than blaming the person for what just happened, it is better to explain how you want things to happen in the future. For example, if a junior person sends something to the client without review, and it contains errors, the tendency is to blame the junior person. She might say (or think) that there were no managers available to review the document or that she just followed the direction she was given. Rather than learning not to do this again, the junior person may feel that it wasn't really her fault.

However, if you approach the conversation by saying, "In the future, I would like to make certain that every document of this type is reviewed by a supervisor before it goes to the client," you have made it clear how you want the junior person to perform in the future without attacking her for the current incident. After all, there is nothing you can do about what just happened. You are merely trying to make certain it doesn't happen next time. You should also explain why it's important to avoid the situation, so the employee is given a fuller picture of how to behave.

As a rule, it is better to create an environment where all employees recognize what they are doing right and where they are making mistakes. They need to feel that they can admit errors without repercussions. This can be done by how you run group meetings after an activity takes place.

In many cases, when something goes right, managers congratulate one another and the staff in e-mails and maybe make an announcement in a larger group meeting. When something goes wrong, we get the group together to figure out what went wrong; in essence, we try to figure out who we should blame. As highlighted on page 51, being blamed makes a person respond defensively and focus on what things outside her control contributed to the problem.

You will get better results if you handle both successes and failures in the same way. After an activity, get the team together. Tell them that the outcome was great, good, fair or poor, and then challenge each of them to share what they could have done differently to make it better next time.

Start with yourself, and then go around the table, asking each person how she could have done some things to improve the outcome. No one can say what another person could have done differently. She can only comment on her own actions. This method allows each person to openly examine how she can improve without the possibility of retribution and helps you grow your production capability painlessly.

If you plan to use this process, explain your intention to your staff beforehand and implement it on one or two successful events before using it on an event that had an issue. If you start with a problem, your employees may feel that it is just another "blame" session.

The language you use will greatly influence how you are perceived and how well you are able to engage with your employees. Words like "always" and "never" should be avoided unless you know that there are no exceptions, which is quite rare. For example, if you say to a staffer,

"You're always late to meetings," it's likely that the employee will focus on the few times she was on time rather than on the times she was late.

In particular, there is one word that should be avoided as much as possible: "but." When you say "but," you are rejecting what the person just said. For example, if an employee suggests that you do something and you say, "Yes, but …," you just turned down her idea, and she is less likely to hear what you have to say next. If, on the other hand, you say "Yes, and…," you can introduce your alternative idea without alienating your staff. Generally, the words "although" and "however" will produce the same result as "but."

Conflict

Conflict among employees, or between you and an employee, is inevitable. People often see the same information and draw different conclusions based on what they observed. Even if they are directly involved in the event, they will filter the observation through their own lenses.

Each person has been raised differently with various influences on their life. As a result, we process information in our own way, based on our own rules and values. This fact can frequently lead to conflict because each party believes she is "right" based on her interpretation of the incident.

Therefore, when trying to mediate conflict, it is important to get past the "interpretations" and get down to the facts.

When you ask a person involved in an argument why she is fighting, you may hear her say something like, "Because what she's saying makes absolutely no sense," but you would never hear her say, "Because what I'm saying makes absolutely no sense."

Both parties believe they are correct. They are not arguing the facts of the incident; they are arguing based on their interpretation of the facts and the effect it had on them. You can see this very clearly when a speech is made by a president or another important political official. You can listen to the speech, which is the event itself, and have an extremely different interpretation of that speech than the person sitting right next to you.

One of the most fun examples was in the movie, *Annie Hall.* Diane Keaton and Woody Allen are having marital issues. They are both seeing therapists. In one scene, on a split screen, you see and hear the following dialogue:

Woody Allen's therapist: "How often do you sleep together?"

Diane Keaton's therapist: "Do you have sex often?"

Woody Allen: "Hardly ever. Maybe three times a week."

Diane Keaton: "Constantly. I'd say three times a week."

They are obviously not arguing about the fact that they are intimate about three times a week. If you were managing this argument, you must get past "hardly ever" and "constantly" and get to "three times a week." They are arguing about what three times a week means to each of them.

When managing conflicts, it's very important to keep certain things in mind. You must avoid immediately offering advice on how to solve the problem. You should paraphrase to make certain that you understand what they are saying and try to understand their motivation; however, you need to challenge the conclusions they've reached. Ask why they believe what they believe. Offer alternative conclusions that might be reached from the same event.

Often, when I coach an individual who has a history of conflict with someone, I will ask, "How would you react if your friend did or said this thing?" After denying that her friend would *ever* do or say that thing, she admits that it wouldn't bother her. It is often connected to how we feel about someone that influences how we respond rather than the action itself.

Two lessons can be learned here. First, people tend to bring baggage into any conflict situation, so you need to help them get past the past and focus on the event under consideration. Second, as the manager, you too have biases about the people in conflict. You need to leave your own baggage home and address the issue at hand.

Listening Skills

One of the most important skills a manager needs to learn is to listen properly. Because we can hear, we think that we can listen, but the two do not necessarily coincide. Hearing is a physical act. Listening is a cognitive event. In fact, not all listening is auditory.

According to the work of Albert Mehrabian, Professor Emeritus of Psychology at UCLA, when dealing with communication involving feelings and attitudes, and when there is incongruence between verbal and nonverbal messages, the words  we speak only acwcount for 7% of our communication. The other 93% comprises tone of voice (38%) and nonverbal behavior (55%).[1] So, you must listen with your ears and your eyes.

It's important to note that if the words spoken do not align with the tone of voice or body language, people will ignore the words and believe the other signals they are receiving. In addition, this disconnect tends to lessen the receiver's trust in the person delivering the information.

---

1. Jeff Thompson, PhD, "Is Nonverbal Communication a Numbers Game?" *Psychology Today* (2011), https://www.psychologytoday.com/us/blog/beyond-words/201109/is-nonverbal-communication-numbers-game.

Some studies[2] have indicated that, in a typical 30-minute conversation between two people, there can be as many as 800 nonverbal messages sent between the participants. A tremendous amount of information can be gleaned from these messages if you pay attention to them.

At many of my sessions, I inquire, "If I ask you a question in English, you will always answer it. Do you agree?" Some will say "yes"; others "no." Some will shake or nod their heads. Some will articulate their response; others will clearly indicate the extent of their agreement with overt body language. Some seemingly do not respond at all, but I point out that every one of them answered the question within their own brains. It's a matter of science.

If I had been carefully watching one of the people who seemingly did not respond at all, I might have been able to pick up on the less obvious facial reactions or body-language clues to understand whether or not she believed my statement.

If you are dealing with a person's feelings or attitudes, it is very important to meet her face to face to have the greatest chance of truly understanding her and making a connection.

One thing often makes it difficult to actually listen to someone: We're too busy listening to our internal voice. We focus on what we want to say next rather than truly listen to what we hear.

We are often eager to jump to a solution when faced with a problem, even before we have fully examined the issue to make certain that we have identified its depth. This approach is equivalent to a doctor prescribing medicine before completely diagnosing a medical problem.

---

2. J. Hargrave, "Do you speak body language?: Mastering the art of nonverbal communication key in interrogations," *The Forensic Examiner*, 17(3) (2008): 17-22, https://psycnet.apa.org/record/2008-11581-001.

To quote the 14th Dalai Lama, "When you talk, you are only repeating what you already know. But, if you listen, you may learn something new."

Communication Styles

Different people communicate differently. There are four basic styles of communication: thinker, feeler, intuitor and sensor. These styles have significant benefits and drawbacks. Most people primarily use one or two styles during normal communication, and many change to a different style when under stress.

It's very important to ascertain what style the person you're speaking with is using at that moment because you will more effectively communicate if you can flex your own style to the same style or at least to something reasonably compatible.

In the following definitions, I will refer to a person as being a thinker, a feeler, an intuitor or a sensor, but it's not that a person *is* one of these things; it's that the person currently is using one of these communication styles. Some people rely on one type more than others, but everyone can access and use other styles.

Thinker

Thinkers are analytical, methodical, rational and objective. They want facts, figures and data to help them decide. They do not typically make quick decisions because they are analyzing the information at hand. As a result, thinkers can be frustrating to those who use other communication styles and look for more rapid decision making.

You can tell if someone is in thinker mode by the way they are communicating. They ask for time to evaluate something. They present informations in an outline or a step-by-step manner. They ask a lot of questions. They provide more background than you may want to hear. They choose their words carefully.

They are generally effective communicators and have a stabilizing effect on the group by providing objective, prudent counsel. However, when taken to an extreme, thinkers can become overly cautious, rigid, unemotional and indecisive.

If you are trying to effectively communicate with someone in thinker mode, you should take the time to walk through your thought process step by step, organize the information sequentially and offer options (pros and cons). Most importantly, you should take your time.

Feeler

Feelers feel. They love human interaction. They care about what others are thinking. As a result, they are empathetic. They read nonverbal feedback very well and notice subtle changes in others' moods. They are frequently good at drawing out the feelings of others and are seen as warm, supportive and comforting.

There are cues you can use to see when someone is in feeler mode. They make good eye contact and are inclined to use your name while speaking. They frequently get close and/or make physical contact. When presented with an idea, they will generally want to know how it will affect other people and/or who else has reviewed the concept. You will find that, because they are sensitive to feelings, they often defend the actions of others.

Because of their ability to relate to others' feelings, they are generally approachable and sought out by people with problems. They are also persuasive and spontaneous. When taken too far, that persuasiveness can become manipulative, and their spontaneity can result in impulsiveness. Because feelers rely on gut rather than on information, they can be subjective or too anecdotal.

To communicate with someone in feeler mode, you will want to make a connection by building rapport, expressing interest or having the discussion over coffee or a meal. When presenting an idea, you should note how others have responded to it and how it will affect whatever groups are involved.

Intuitor

Intuitor behavior is rarer than the other three. Intuitors are very creative and comfortable with theory and grand concepts. They are innovative, original and imaginative. They are always looking at the big picture.

They focus on the future and want to create something that has never been done before. They're not interested in what restrictions might make it difficult to achieve.

When someone is in intuitor mode, they are not concerned with how their ideas will be implemented and may even articulate ideas that are not possible. This approach often makes it difficult for other styles that are more focused on the process. However, you can make the case that every manmade thing in our world was first conceptualized in the mind of someone in intuitor mode.

Because they are not concerned with details, when communicating with intuitors you need to focus on the future and the unique nature of your idea.

Sensor

Sensors are action and results oriented. They can be impatient and hurried, working on multiple projects simultaneously. They can be very productive because they are continually looking to move projects forward.

They are not interested in chit chat and want to get to the matter at hand as quickly as possible. They can be hard-charging and ride roughshod over others as they drive the process forward.

To deal with someone in sensor mode, you need to be extremely results oriented and minimize anything that is not directly related to the matter at hand.

Although sensors tend to get things done, they often anger others who predominantly use other communications styles. They push for action before thinkers are ready, and they're not interested in others' feelings along the way. Interestingly, many people who operate primarily in other styles morph to sensor when they are under stress.

One final note on communication styles: For maximum effective communication, it is best to try to flex your style to something compatible to the style being used by the other person. Generally speaking, this means matching their style; however, you should at least try to avoid certain combinations. For example, thinkers and feelers do not usually communicate well with sensors or intuitors.

Delegation

One thing that plagues many agencies is the inability of supervisors and managers to delegate properly. This situation has significant financial implications, which we will cover later (see page 70), but it also has an enormous influence on the performance of the agency.

As employees move up in the organization, they are promoted based on the work they are doing at each level. They learn new skills closely related to those they already do well and get the next promotion.

Then, at some point, they are promoted to a supervisory position. The skills for this position are different from anything they have experienced before. They will no longer be judged on what they do but on what the people under them do.

In addition to not receiving training to get the most out of others, their own success is now determined by how others perform. It's no wonder that many of these employees have difficulty letting go.

The more senior person can typically complete assignments quicker than the people reporting to her because she has more experience. So, to get things done quickly, managers will frequently give the task to the person who knows how to do it.

When that happens, the supervisor continues to do work she already knows how to do and does not have time to learn anything new. In addition, the more junior employee does not get the opportunity to learn the new task. The agency essentially stagnates as no new learning takes place.

Therefore, it makes more sense to have the person who knows the skill teach the more inexperienced employee. There are several benefits to this approach:

- The junior employee learns a new skill, allowing her to expand her capabilities and move on a trajectory to a new level.
- The supervisor no longer handles this task, freeing up her time to also learn new skills.
- The agency now has two employees who are capable of effectively handling this type of assignment, which doubles the production capacity.
- The cost of doing the work is reduced, which is reflected in lower overservicing and higher profits on the account. This will be covered in more detail later (see page 70).

It's very important to teach your supervisors how to manage staff effectively. When they are responsible for an activity, their first thought should be, "Who needs to learn how to do this?" They should use the work to develop the staff rather than use the staff to do the work.

When assigning a project to a more junior employee, there is a process that should be followed to increase the likelihood of success.

At the start, the assignment should be put into context within the surrounding program. The employee may be faced with decisions about how to handle certain activities while working on a task. If she has a clear understanding of how that task fits into the bigger picture, she is more likely to decide on her own rather than come back to the supervisor to solve the problem.

It's critically important that there is a clear definition and understanding of the deliverable. Very often, supervisors give what they think is a clear explanation, but the employee hears something different or interprets it in some other way. To make certain they are both on the same page, the supervisor should have the employee repeat the assignment in her own words. This will greatly increase the chance that the finished product will meet the expectations of the supervisor.

Before leaving the delegation session, the parties should agree on follow-up steps and intermediate deadlines. If the employee has limited experience with this specific type of assignment, they should set more frequent check-ins to ensure that the process is staying on track.

Don't assume that any of your supervisors and managers have the requisite skills to handle staff. Developing management and leadership skills; understanding the motivation triggers; handling praise, criticism and conflict; and delegating effectively are all skills they may not have needed before you put them in charge of staff. Carefully monitor their development in these areas and bring in trainers or coaches to help them, if needed. Their ability to manage effectively is extremely important to the overall success of your agency.

Paying Your Employees Properly

Based on studies that we have done, there are many instances where the best employees at a given level are paid less than others at that level. Although this doesn't make sense, it happens often and should be evaluated regularly.

Here's the scenario that makes it happen:

Ann starts working for you as an assistant account executive. She is a good employee, and over the next 10 years she is promoted to an account executive, a senior account executive, and then an account supervisor. She typically receives 5% raises, so her annual salary has risen from $35,000 to more than $57,000.

Five years after she starts, Barbara starts to work for you as an assistant account executive. She is clearly a star, and after five years she has also risen to the level of account supervisor. She received much better raises than Ann, averaging 8% per year. However, because it has taken only five years, she is now being paid a little more than $51,000.

In this situation, you are at risk of losing a much better employee to your competitors and keeping the more expensive employee with less upside potential. We strongly recommend that you take specific steps to guard against this possibility.

Set salary ranges for each position. These ranges should overlap slightly. Then, when a person gets a promotion to a new level, she should get a raise to at least the bottom salary set for that position. This situation may require that the person receives a raise of 15% or 20% or more, but that approach will reward the employee fairly and guard against the scenario above.

A second benefit of salary ranges is that marginal employees, who receive less frequent promotions, may bump up against the top end of the range. When this happens, they should only receive raises consistent with a change in the range due to inflation until they are ready for the next promotion.

This approach will widen the range of salary increase percentages but will help you invest in, and keep, your best employees.

Additional Compensation

In addition to salary, many agencies reward employees at the end of the year based on the performance of the company or the individual performance of the employee.

When you merely give each employee a percentage of her salary based on the performance of the company, it is more like profit sharing than a bonus plan. Under a plan like this, you should set goals for the agency that the employees can influence and share them with the staff. It should be clear that the better the agency performs against those goals, the higher the reward for the employees.

For more senior personnel, you may want to implement a metrics-driven bonus program. You need to determine what behavior you want to encourage from your managers and develop a bonus program that rewards success in those areas. Some possible examples are new business development, client retention or growth, overservicing levels, employee utilization levels, employee retention and group profitability. When developing this plan, you should pay attention to things that can be manipulated and make certain to include something that is a counterbalance to that element. For example, if you focus on overservicing, you should also include a measurement on employee utilization. Without it, if the manager encourages people to stay within the budget, they may still work the hours but not record them in the time-tracking system.

Bonus systems can be tricky. If you are not certain about how to set up one effectively, you should consult with an expert to help you develop it. If you don't, you may create a program that encourages behavior counter to your goals.

Building and Maintaining Profitability

Rule number one: Never lose money. Rule number two: Never forget rule number one.

—Warren Buffett

A s James C. Collins and Jerry I. Porras state in *Built to Last*, "Profitability is a necessary condition for existence and a means to more important ends, but it is not the end in itself for many of the visionary companies. Profit is like oxygen, food, water and blood for the body; they are not the point of life, but without them, there is no life."[3]

If you would like to achieve everything we've covered up to this point, it is critical that you run your business like a business and focus on achieving long-term financial success. In this section, we will examine many important components contributing to this goal.

Critical Ratios

Most agencies strive to achieve a profit margin between 15% and 20%. In most cases, to attain that level of profit, they must keep their total compensation costs between 57% and 62% of revenue. Compensation costs include payroll, benefits, payroll taxes and freelance costs. This allows 7–8% for facilities, 2–3% for marketing expenses and 11–13% for other expenses.

It's clear that the only way to achieve the profit you desire is to make certain that you can generate enough revenue for each dollar of salary. You need leverage. The factors that influence this are how much you pay each employee, what percentage of each person's time is billable and how much overservicing you incur.

Industry data will guide you regarding how much to pay employees at every level, in every geography and in each practice. In addition, yearly statistics regarding the average billable percentages and billing

---

3. James C. Collins and Jerry I. Porras, *Built to Last* (New York: Harper Collins Publishers, 1994). 55.

rates for each level are available. With the proper mix of staff, these averages will put you on the right path to make a reasonable profit.

However, the final step in the process is to actually bill and collect for a substantial portion of the time that's logged to client programs. You must keep overservicing to a minimum.

Overservicing

If you're paying your employees correctly and setting proper billing rates and billable targets, and your employees come close to their targets, you are nearly assured of reasonable margins—provided, of course, that you keep overservicing in check.

Overservicing is not just lost revenue. If you overservice a client by 10%, when you return to the office after Thanksgiving, you will be working for the rest of the year for that client for nothing. If your overservicing reaches 20%, you are not being paid for your work for all of November and December. At 30%, you are giving away the entire fourth quarter, and at 40% nearly all the time after Labor Day is free to the client.

This is unfair to your agency and to your employees. Because of the effect overservicing has on your bottom line, it will negatively influence your ability to reward your staff.

If you think about it another way, when overservicing reaches 20–30%, you are essentially reducing the billing rate of each level to the level below it. For example, if someone logs 20 hours at $200 an hour, the total billable time is $4,000. If you can only collect $3,200, it equates to that employee billing at $160 an hour.

Many factors contribute to overservicing. Our research indicates that the single most significant component of this problem is employees doing work that could be done by someone at a more junior level. In presentations to more than 100 agencies, whenever we ask if anyone is "doing work below their pay grade," most of the attendees raise their hand.

This situation typically happens because an employee is working on a client's program and, over time, gets promoted. The client likes working with the employee, so there is great reluctance to take the person off the account. However, with each raise, the profit on the account is reduced and, with every promotion, the overservicing increases.

It is very important to address this issue on an ongoing basis. The client/agency relationship cannot be dependent on a single person. It is imperative to connect with the client at multiple levels, so when it is time to move an employee to another project, the relationship remains strong.

When faced with the prospect of having to move an important person off an account, you should address it directly with the client. Explain that the work on the account is below the level of the person working on it. In other words, you can say, "The work was done by this person when she was an account executive and should be done by an account executive today."

Further, if the client likes the employee, you can appeal to the fact that it's in the employee's best interest to learn new things and grow and that the employee deserves higher pay and promotions. Without those incentives, the employee may leave and will be lost to both the client and the agency.

You may have better luck with this discussion if you use it as an alternative to charging more money to cover the overservicing. The conversation might be something like, "We've been overservicing your business by about 25% each month. We need to find a way to get the service more in line with the amount of the retainer. We propose that we increase the retainer by X%. Alternatively, we can change the staff mix on the account by giving Barbara more time and reducing Carol's hours."

By providing the client with two choices, both of which are acceptable to you, you give the client the option of deciding which one fits their need best. The threat of increased cost may help make the employee switch more palatable.

A second significant cause of overservicing is "scope creep" where the agency is asked to do things during the month that were not in the original scope of work. The only way to effectively protect yourself from this problem is to have a well-defined scope of work that details what is included and what is *excluded* in the program.

Then, when something is requested that falls outside the scope, you have the option of raising the issue with the client to discuss whether the budget should be increased or whether other activities can be reduced or eliminated.

Managing Retainers

The issue of scope creep is more pronounced on retainer accounts because they are frequently not built on the basis of budgeting specific activities but more likely on a "gut feel" of what it will take to "do the job" and/or what the client is willing to pay.

Retainers have some advantages over other billing arrangements. They are excellent for cash flow and easy for the client to understand. In terms of cash flow, you can invoice the client at the start of the month, or earlier, and therefore receive payment close to the time you incur expenses. In contrast, when you bill the actual time you spent during the month, you must wait for the month to end, collect the data, put the invoice together and double-check the amount. This is generally at least five to six weeks later than a retainer invoice would be sent for the same period. It may also take the client longer to pay because they must review the time spent rather than having an invoice of a specific, agreed-upon amount.

However, although you are billing the client the same amount each month, that is not a reflection of the work you will do each month. The amount of time spent each month will be determined by the activities being worked on and the number of days in the month. The activities you are committed to execute each month will determine how much time will be spent. Even if you do the same amount of work every day, there will be great fluctuation in the amount of time logged. Monthly billable days generally range from 19 to 23, depending on weekends and holidays. That means that you will log 21% more time in a 23-day month than you will in a 19-day month.

You should not fall into the trap of thinking that you should be staffing each account based on the amount of the retainer. In fact, you should resist the urge to use the terminology "retainer." If you have a client that is paying you $10,000 per month, this is a $120,000 annual program.

It is best to build the annual budget by budgeting each activity and adding them together to come up with the total budget. You can then suggest to the client that you would be happy to divide the budget by 12 and invoice the same amount each month. The advantage of presenting it this way is two-fold. You will better identify the specific activities that the budget covers and educate the client regarding how the time may be spent each month.

For example, in the chart below, you will see a $20,000 per month retainer creating a $240,000 annual budget. Let's assume that in general the program calls for consistent work being done each day. However, the client will be announcing a new product in May and attend a trade show in September. These are separate activities that will take place at specific times of the year and will require a considerable amount of time during those months.

Month	Billing ($)	Spikes ($)	Billable Days	Staffing Levels ($)
Jan	20,000	14,000	21	14,067
Feb	20,000	14,000	19	12,727
Mar	20,000	14,000	22	14,737
Apr	20,000	14,000	21	14,067
May	20,000	40,000	22	40,000
Jun	20,000	14,000	21	14,067
Jul	20,000	14,000	20	13,397
Aug	20,000	14,000	23	15,407
Sep	20,000	60,000	19	60,000
Oct	20,000	14,000	23	15,407
Nov	20,000	14,000	20	13,397
Dec	20,000	14,000	19	12,727
Total	240,000	240,000	250	240,000

As the chart indicates, you need to set aside $40,000 for the work in May and $60,000 for the work in September. Therefore, $100,000 of the $240,000 program will be spent in two months, leaving only $140,000 to be spread over the 10 months of the rest of the year (roughly $14,000 per month). If the work done each day is consistent, the amount spent in each month will range from a low of under $13,000 to nearly $15,500 based on the number of billable days in each month.

If you go through this exercise and create a similar chart, you can easily explain to the client how you expect to spend the budget for the year. Then, as you log the actual time, you can compare it to what was anticipated and act, if needed. For example, let's assume that you show this information to the client, and they agree that it makes sense. In January, you bill the client $20,000 and spend $18,000 in time. You did not *under*service this by $2,000; you *over*serviced it by nearly $4,000. You will need to determine if you will service it less in subsequent months or accept the $4,000 loss.

Your time-management software needs to track servicing in this way. It should automatically increase or decrease the amount available to spend in subsequent months based on what has already been spent to date and what is anticipated going forward. If you would like a demonstration of how that should work, please contact me.

Simply comparing spending each month to the amount billed will lead to lack of control and potentially significant losses.

We believe it is best to keep the client aware of how much was spent each month and year to date versus the anticipated spending in the original forecast on the chart. If you find that you are continually overspending as compared to the chart, and you are keeping the client informed regarding the increasing overage, after a few months you can approach the client to discuss ways in which you can bring spending more in line with the budget.

As before, when approaching a client about an overage and presenting ways to reduce overservicing, it is always best to present options to having the client pay more. As stated earlier (see page 70), you may be able to suggest that some of the work be moved to a more junior person. Other options might include eliminating some nonvalue-added reports or activities, reducing the frequency or number of attendees at meetings or having personnel on the client side execute some of the tasks you are currently working on. The goal is to get time worked better aligned with the budget by getting paid more or executing work more efficiently.

Managing Freelancers

There are times when you need to reach outside your staff to get work completed for your clients. You may need specific skills your employees don't have, or you may have too much work at that moment. There is nothing wrong with this process provided you are handling it correctly.

Freelancers should be treated as surrogate staff. Their costs should be included in your agency's compensation section, and they should fill out time sheets and have them entered into your time-tracking system.

Your time-management software needs to track servicing in this way. It should automatically increase or decrease the amount available to spend in subsequent months based on what has already been spent to date and what is anticipated going forward. If you would like a demonstration of how that should work, please contact me.

Simply comparing spending each month to the amount billed will lead to lack of control and potentially significant losses.

Of course, when you use freelancers you are increasing your costs. So, if you are using them because of a particularly heavy workload, it's always best to first look internally and see if there are overservicing hours that can be reduced on other clients, freeing up time from your staff that you are already paying for.

Client Budgeting

As stated earlier (see page 72), client budgets should be built from the ground up, depending on the specific needs of the client and the program elements that will help them achieve their goals. Very often, we lock into a price before we even know what we will be doing for the client.

Most agencies have a minimum retainer that they are willing to accept and, in an attempt to verify that the prospect can afford to work with them, they state that minimum on the initial call. Our research shows that most clients fall within 10–15% of an agency's minimum. In other words, once you tell them that your minimum is $10,000 per month, in most cases that will anchor the size of the budget you receive.

Instead of talking about minimums or monthly amounts, you may want to address a cost question by saying something like, "The size of the budget is dependent on the activities we believe will help you achieve your goals, so it's difficult to price it until we develop a strategic plan and program for you. However, based on what we've discussed so far, a program for you might range between $120,000 and $350,000 per year. We can, of course, bill you in equal monthly amounts if that works best for you."

In this way, you are clearly making sure that they have enough money because the low end is in line with your minimum; however, you now have a much broader range to revisit once the program is developed.

In fact, by developing the budget with specific activities, you can give them a budget for a core program at the lower end and show what else they can achieve by adding other elements. Very often, clients will agree to an increase in the original budget if there are additional elements that they feel will enhance the effectiveness of the program.

Pricing

Many clients may ask for or demand a discount off your regular rates, and you may feel compelled to give it to them to win or keep the account. This is a decision that should not be made in haste.

If you feel that you must provide the discount, see if you can get something in return. For example, maybe you can get a larger portion of the client's communications program, introductions to other business units/client products or more favorable payment terms.

Generally, the larger clients will put you in this position, so the effect on your agency is greater. As an example, if you give a 10% discount to a client that represents 10% of your business, you will drop a full percentage point of profit. If that client is 25% of the total business for a specific practice, that 10% discount will make it much more difficult for that practice to achieve the targets you've set for each part of your business. In any case, in order to get back to the goals you've set, the discount you've given one client will force you, unfairly, to make higher margins on other accounts.

Regardless of how you price your work, you must be very specific in how you define the scope of work that's included and *excluded* from the budget to fight scope creep.

Income Recognition

The purpose of reviewing your financial results each month is to help you determine whether your agency is improving over time. How your financial person records income and expenses is critical in providing you with information that can help you make the right decisions.

Income and expenses should be aligned each month. In other words, you should take income and recognize expenses in the month the work is performed. This is known as an accrual method of accounting as opposed to a cash-basis method.

On a cash basis, income is not recognized until the client pays the bill. Since the work is done one month and the invoice is paid another month, there is no alignment. In fact, there are often payments for several months' work received in the same month, creating large swings in income that reflect the timing of payments but not the performance of the agency.

On an accrual basis, revenue for retainers should be recognized in the month the work is done and billed in the same month, so a bill for $10,000 on March 1 would cover the work for March. For project work, however, the income should be recognized equally over the time of the project or based on how much time is expended each month. For example, if you bill a client in March for a $24,000 project that is expected to take four months, you should recognize $6,000 per month for March, April, May and June. This will more closely align the income to the employee costs for each month.

On a final note, even if your taxes are done on a cash basis, your management books must be done on an accrual basis to provide you with the information you need to make the correct decisions.

Expense Recognition

Just like income, expenses should be carefully monitored to be aligned with each month. Significant costs, like rent and payroll, must always be expensed in the correct month.

If you pay your employees every two weeks, there will be 26 paychecks each year. Over the course of 12 months, there will be 10 months with two paychecks and two months with three paychecks. This scenario makes it appear that your performance is better than it is for 10 months and worse than it is for two months.

To easily remedy this situation, you can move your pay periods to twice per month. Although there will be two fewer paychecks per year, each one will be larger, and your expenses will be more accurately reflected.

Another area that causes significant distortion to financial results and masks actual performance is reimbursable expenses and cost of goods sold (COGS). Once again, alignment is critical. You need to take the COGS the same month as you recognized the income through billing, preferably during the month that the work was done.

Without this discipline, you will have very high gross profit the month you billed the client and very low (or negative) gross profit the month the COGS is recognized. It will be difficult to determine whether your agency is making progress and may cloud your ability to make proper decisions regarding staffing and other investments.

Billing Power

One of the first analyses you should undertake is a billing-power analysis. Basically, this is the litmus test to determine how much revenue you could potentially generate if all employees reached their billable targets and you were able to bill every hour logged.

The calculation is straightforward. For each level, multiply the billing rate for that level by the total hours for the year by the billable target for the level by the number of employees at that level. Then add the totals from each calculation.

Level	Billing Rate ($)	Total Hours	Billable Target	Number of Employees	Total ($)
Level 1	125	1,750	95%	4	831,250
Level 2	150	1,750	90%	4	945,000
Level 3	180	1,750	80%	3	756,000
Level 4	225	1,750	75%	2	590,625
Level 5	275	1,750	60%	1	288,750
Total				**14**	**3,411,625**

In the example above, the standard hours are 1,750. This reflects a 9:00 a.m. to 5:00 p.m. workplace, calculated at 40 hours per week times 52 weeks, equaling 2,080 hours. In most cases, there are roughly 10 holidays, or 80 hours, so the available time is 2,000 hours. There are 250 workdays times eight hours per day. With one hour for lunch each day, we subtract 250 hours and get 1,750 hours.

If you are open from 8:30 a.m. to 5:00 p.m., or from 9:00 a.m. to 5:30 p.m., you would use 1,875 hours as your standard; if you are open from 8:00 a.m. to 5:00 p.m., or from 9:00 a.m. to 6:00 p.m., you would use 2,000 hours as your standard. In those instances, you should adjust the billable targets to take the increased time into account.

While it would be nice for the agency above to achieve $3.4 million in revenue, the reality is that it would be nearly impossible to do so. Some employees will not achieve their billable targets, and there will inevitably be some overservicing. While the amount may vary from one agency to the next, in most cases your billing power will need to be more than the revenue you need to achieve your margins. You can typically expect to make 75–80% of your billing power. In other words, the agency above should expect to generate between $2.5 million and $2.75 million in revenue related to time.

Agency Structure

It's important that you manage your staffing mix appropriately. In most public relations practices, there is greater leverage with more junior employees. There are two reasons for this.

As an employee moves into supervisory and management positions, more time is spent on marketing, new business and administrative activities, and generally those employees get more vacation time. Therefore, there are fewer potential billable hours, and their billable targets are lower. While this is one contributing factor to the issue, it is not the most significant component. More importantly, salaries rise more rapidly than billing rates. For example, an employee making $40,000 per year may have a billing rate of $120 per hour. As she rises in the organization, she may eventually earn $80,000, and the billing rate for that level might be $180 per hour.

In this case, the salary has increased by 100% and the billing rate by 50%. This is typical. If you examine the return on each person in the chart below, you can see that there is little change in the amount of revenue generated by each level ($200,000 to $308,000, which is 54% more from bottom to top), but the personnel at Level 4 make nearly three times more than the employees at the entry-level position.

Level	Salary ($)	Rate ($)	Target	Revenue ($)	Ratio
Level 1	110,000	220	80%	308,000	2.80
Level 2	85,000	180	85%	267,750	3.15
Level 3	65,000	160	90%	252,000	3.88
Level 4	40,000	120	95%	199,500	4.99
Total	300,000			1,027,250	

In most cases, you would want to try to achieve a ratio of billable personnel salaries to potential revenue of 3.5 or more in order to achieve a reasonable profit percentage. However, as you can see, the ratio is different for each level based on billable targets and the ratio between the salary and the billing rate.

The ratio is higher for more junior personnel and lower as the employee moves up the ranks. This concept is important because, if the ratio of senior to junior employees changes, it can make profitability difficult to achieve.

The schematic above shows a fairly typical agency structure with two very senior people at the top and then four at the next level, six at the next, eight at the next and 10 at the entry level. Under this scenario, if billing rates, billable targets and salaries are set correctly and if over-servicing is kept under control, it is reasonable to assume that the ratio of salary to revenue will produce a profitable agency.

However, over time, employees will learn new skills and move up in the hierarchy. After a short period, maybe one person at each of the four lowest levels gets promoted, so the structure now looks like this:

The salary-to-revenue ratio at each higher level is less than the level below it, so the salary costs rise while revenue remains constant. In addition, as each employee is promoted, the value of each of the hours she logs is more, so overservicing increases as well.

After another round of promotions, the structure looks more like a box than a triangle (see below schematic), and profitability is extremely difficult, if not impossible.

This is a common occurrence among agencies. It is especially true in those agencies that engender longevity by creating an environment people like and don't want to leave and where management is reluctant to act on poor performers. Over time, this can create situations where many people are working on assignments that should be handled by more junior personnel because there are not enough juniors to pass the work down to.

In most cases, you should strive to maintain a pyramidical structure. To do this, and still provide growth opportunities to your employees, you must generate enough top-line growth to continue to add new employees at the lower levels. This approach allows you to maintain the structure, keep the average salary constant despite giving raises and provide the correct personnel to handle each assignment.

Firing Clients

One of the most difficult things for an agency to do is fire a client. No one wants to give up revenue, but this is one of the most important things you can do to maintain a healthy, profitable company.

There are many reasons to consider firing a client:

- They may continually add assignments and be unwilling to discuss compensating you for the additional work.
- They may insist on additional cost reductions that will make profitability more difficult.
- They may be overly hard on your employees.
- They may not respect weekend or nighttime boundaries.
- They may not heed your counsel.

Some of these issues have an immediate effect on your profit; others may cause more long-term effects. If your employees are unhappy working with a particular client, it can take a tremendous toll on employee morale and retention.

The least painful way to terminate a relationship with a client is when you win a new account that is similar in size, or larger, than the one you want to jettison. You will slow your growth but improve your margins and offer a better place to work.

You should always keep a list of which clients you feel you would terminate first if the situation presents itself. That way, you can take action when you need to.

Conclusion

Success depends on previous preparation, and
without such preparation there is sure to be failure.

—Confucius

R
unning an agency can be a daunting task, requiring the owner to excel in areas other than communications including talent management, financial acumen, systems analysis and sales. Most agency owners did not enter the business to focus on these areas, but, as noted in this book, they are necessary to be successful over the long term.

Smart owners will hire individuals who can complement their skill set in the areas that are needed. Many owners look to outside consultants with industry experience to provide guidance and processes to make the job easier and less painful.

I hope this book has provided some helpful information to make you think differently about your business. If I can be of further assistance on these issues, please do not hesitate to contact me for guidance or recommendations to others who may help.

Darryl Salerno
914-737-1222
darryl@secondquadrant.com
www.secondquadrant.com
www.staffallocationsolution.com

Made in USA - North Chelmsford, MA
1062656_9780578633961
03.25.2020 1223